Down and Up

EST. 75 1938
YEARS
THE UNIVERSITY OF GEORGIA PRESS 2013

Down and Up

Poems by Clarence Major

The University of Georgia Press
Athens & London

Published by the University of Georgia Press
Athens, Georgia 30602
www.ugapress.org
© 2013 by Clarence Major
All rights reserved
Set in 10/15 Garamond Premier Pro
Printed and bound by Sheridan Books Inc.

The paper in this book meets the guidelines for
permanence and durability of the Committee on
Production Guidelines for Book Longevity of the
Council on Library Resources.

Printed in the United States of America

17 16 15 14 13 P 5 4 3 2 1

Library of Congress Cataloging-in-Publication Data

Major, Clarence.
  [Poems. Selections]
  Down and up : poems / by Clarence Major.
    pages ; cm.
  ISBN 978-0-8203-4594-9 (pbk. : alk. paper) —
  ISBN 0-8203-4594-6 (pbk. : alk. paper)
  I. Title.
  PS3563.A39D69 2013
  811'.54—dc23

                              2013009172

British Library Cataloging-in-Publication Data available

Contents

Acknowledgments

"Down and Up," *Harvard Review*, no. 37 (Fall/Winter 2009).

"Self and Self," *Eleven Eleven*, no. 9 (2010).

"Bride Stripped Bare," "The Unknown," "We Have Yet," and "Writing Poetry," *Clarence Major / Myself Painting* (exhibition catalogue), Terre Haute: University Art Gallery, Center for Performing and Fine Arts, Indiana State University, 2011.

"On Watching a Caterpillar Become a Butterfly," © 1994 by Clarence Major reprinted from *African American Review* 28, no. 1 (Spring 1994). Reprinted by permission of Clarence Major.

Down and Up

Writing Poetry

In front of the bishop and me
a blind man with a white stick
walking up a path alongside
the stone wall above the river,
beating the earth rhythmically,
a metrical beat,
carefully placing one foot
in front of the other.
Strong stress, weak stress,
repeating the pattern.
A pattern surely, step by step.
Bapbap du bap!
Occasionally tapping the wall
to make sure it's still there.
In his rhythm yet not,
deliberately slower,
as not to overtake him,
the bishop and I talking
to the same beat,
our words taken away
by the wind high
over the wall.

Bride Stripped Bare

(after Duchamp)

When in transit the window glass broke,
she shook and came down
from her wire-web hammock
to make sure
none of her men had had a stroke.
She stopped spastic before them,
in suspended animation,
took a deep breath.
Ten men at a door
in motionlessness. Bachelors all,
largely asleep
extended above
what otherwise might have been
a real bed—or an ocean.

The Forgiven Knife

When we lived there,
they said that

at the river love
seduces innocence.

But who is in the water,
floating on the bottom?

A peasant, she is a fruit seller in a red dress
carrying her basket of fruit

against her belly. She is pleasant.
Escaping the politeness of the man

wearing the pleated dickey,
she brings with her the happy goat,

the goalpost from the last game,
the forgiven knife of the insane man,

brings them all to the kitchen table
with the apples and onions,

but who will fish the body
from the river and honor its life?

Down and Up

Once up, nude or not,
they tend to come down—
gravity not withstanding,
with or without understanding.
They come down.
The woman carrying a lantern
comes down slowly,
inspecting the dark.
A woman fresh from her bath
comes down, damp and refreshed.
Somebody's niece or wife, in a chemise,
stands up and walks down the steps,
each one squeaking under her weight.
Two guards bring down an old woman
seated in a chair. Two boys
carry a woman, asleep in her bed, down slowly.
For the sake of art,
another woman, nursing her baby, comes down.
A man descends while reading a book
about sin and redemption.
They all come down,
down,
down
where everybody else is waiting to ascend.

2   THE UNASCENDED STAIRCASE

No one is going up—yet.
The Calvinist minister must first finish her sermon.
The old woman with one shoe must stand up.
The man refinishing antique furniture
will try his luck when he finishes.
The bejeweled wealthy woman
may be too heavy for the staircase.
She stands on the landing,
inspecting the first step for its sturdiness.
Here is a young woman,
a pimple on the tip of her nose,
skeptical eyes, tight lips,
dimples, and fat cheeks.
She's waiting for her intended.
They are intent on moving
one way or two ways.

The Forest

I love the silence
here in the hills north of Boulder,

in this dark, densely wooded forest.
After a snowstorm, a pine silence.

You feel a dry chill
that is so cold it is actually warm.

This morning I saw a redbird
so red it was blindingly red

against the white snow.
It landed lightly on a limb.

As he touched down,
a soft spray of white flakes fanned out

with no wind to scatter them
as they fell slowly, slowly

and came to rest
on an endless bed of blue snow,

disappearing into that blueness,
as the redbird, looking from side to side,

flicked its tail while
deciding on his next move.

Spring and All

For WCW

Holding a black umbrella overhead
    she's coming slowly down
    the long stairway
    of sandstone
    from the high road
    to the low city
    of cheap shops.

In the bric-a-brac,
    among the breakables,
    a man playing a piano.
She takes off her clothes,
    piles them on the piano.
The shopkeeper's raised eyebrows
    are wheelbarrows
    full of cabbage.
She throws her hips,
    gliding across the floor.
The shopkeeper says,
    "Must be the first day of spring."

On Vacation

Shadows of the season
sticking to surfaces.

We reach the aqueduct.
Nuns walking in twos.

We pass a skull in a window.
I give it a name.

We stand aside for a funeral march.
It marches by.

We sidestep a girl
with a killer dog on a shaky leash.

Before going back
we stop to shoot the ruins.

Subject for a Ballad

. . . or many years later you say,
So that's why
she said what she said,
or you may never know
because she died without telling you,
then again she may have put in it a letter
or, better, told someone, anyone,
who might die before telling you.
Very able, but who could forget
her barley whiskey breath?
Always embarrassed there
by our arguments at the table.
Broom or no broom, she had real class.
Always she left the room,
or at least she left her chair.
You could find her in the kitchen always able
scrubbing grit or polishing a glass.

We Have Yet

In its original state the odalisque
out by the pool
matched the candlesticks
on the Turkish stool.
In its original state
the Minotaur
watching over our money
in a jar looked the same
as the bull ready to charge.
In its original state our sleeplessness
was kin to the pull of our nightmares.
In their original state all things intersecting
were the same as all things crisscrossing.
In its original state the square
was equal to the circle.
In its original state bliss was wed to kiss.
In its original state the bright beauty
of the world through the window
was equal to the serenity inside.

At the Movies

No real person will die in the dark this afternoon.
Many will pretend to die, pretend to ascend.
But the tendency of the body is to fall.
It is only here that we leave our bodies,
levitate up to the big screen
for a temporary weightless life.
We can choose our scenes
and our degree of participation.
They've gathered in large groups
listening to men shouting through bullhorns.
Holy men lifting tiny adults to their bosoms.
We expect tears and swooning.
A dancing nurse
jumping across the clinic floor.
A violinist playing chamber music.
We get more than we expect.
Medics bringing the wounded soldiers
down from the hills on stretchers.
Far out in the ocean
a lone swimmer doing backstrokes.
People in high box seats
shouting insults down at the diva.
A stage full of dancing women
in red dresses doing high kicks.
A man on a train
watching the scenery shooting by
while planning his murder.
A procession of priests and altar boys
marching piously into the cathedral.
A mob dragging a man through a village.
A detective searching a landfill

for the clue, kicking aside a wet mattress,
a rusty car fender, a pile of rotting dresses,
a rusty stroller. Then there it is, *the* clue.
A car chase through bumper-to-bumper traffic.
And there is that moment
when, between crates of fruit
stacked shoulder high, the harlequins
meet unexpectedly,
like Bud and Lou,
startled by each other's presence.
A cloud hides the moon.
The castle in the distance
is almost certainly locked.
An agent chases a Corot thief
flat-footedly through the Louvre.
The Louvre is surrounded.
All the docked boats are off limits.
One streetlight in this darkness
is not enough to show the way.

The Hand

As in a dream he reaches down in the stream
at the image

of his own hand reaching down.

He tries again and once more.
Fog settles heavily over the countryside.

Under the setting sun in a bed of fog
the other hand comes up to meet its other.

The Rope

Let's follow the rope to where it takes us.
Lifesaver or hanging noose.
Roped off or roped in.
We depend on it.
Don't get distracted.
When we get there, take one end,
and I'll take the other.
Ignore the children
in sacks jumping around on the beach.
Don't get distracted by the blue trees,
the floating gulls, the busy sky. Keep walking;
stay close. We'll pass through
a silent city under white moonlight.
Pick up the pace. Ignore the piles of snow,
the crowing rooster. Boot prints
leading to that barn. The farmer's wife
in there killing a goose for dinner.
We're almost there. Boy pulling off his shirt,
making a turban. Over that hill a village
snowed in for the winter. Red Cross workers
can't get back in there till spring.
No one here was ever found guilty.
No one was up to it.
Even when tanks rolled through the city.
Seagulls perched on the ledge of that house.
Everyone in the casino has a scheme.
We now cross a pattern of planks.
People in boats are remote,
but we can still see them—even from here.
Everyone will soon gather at the dinner table

under a glowing chandelier. Cows
up to the shelter. There they go.
People walking across a stone bridge.
Others forbidden to cross.
No records are kept. Whitewashed pier,
six in the morning.
This is the way it is.
That was the way it was.
The shops are closed. A man in a blue suit
crosses the street. Rarely seen,
and always in a flash, the black stallion.
He knows when the flood is coming,
takes to higher ground.
We must not lose confidence.
A storm may be coming in.
We've lived through storms before.
We can survive.
Even armless, unguarded, we'll get there.
The rope will lead us there.
What to do with the eggs in the basket?
Rembrandt down in the cellar
with the slaughtered ox. The musicians
on stage ready to perform. Waiters
tall in yellow and black. A girl walking calmly
with books firmly against her bosom.
Here is my end of the rope.
This is your end.
Now that we are here let us look
back at where we were.

Time and Objects

Ladders to books on top shelves.

Flowers pressed between the pages of old books.

A twin set of stone harlequins
on an end table collecting dust.

An ancient tambourine
on a hook by the fireplace
where fire has never been.

Things endowed with their own language.

Summer Afternoon

Carriages lined up in Central Park waiting for tourists.
Two old men on a bench talking about a knee operation.
The ghost of Frank O'Hara on his lunch break
dashing off a poem. Ladies in pairs, bone thin
and veiled, like figures out of nineteenth-century Paris,
wearing diamond rings, leaving a trail of perfume.
Hippies and junkies beating tambourines.
Harris alone in his loft learning to paint.
And what happened to Mike's sardines?

Houses

There are houses where we've slept and wept,
made love and felt safe,
sorted through piles of papers.
If a vision came after the sermon
in the green house above the bend in the road,
we missed it, missed the vision.
They say the place is blessed and tested.
In one house all morning
I watched a cat watching a bug
on the outside of the window.
On the rug in the study of the gray house
we came upon a dead mouse.
Rails ran by one house like arrows
on a map leading to a Gothic edifice.
The little house in Copenhagen
had no toilet, but we coped.
We hoped for better and got it.
In Venice we lived near one of many cathedrals,
and I always knew ahead of time
when the bells were going to ring.
In Martinique in a little cottage
we played poker into the wee hours.
A unique time by a singing sea.
Our friend Ernest slept in a room
where he could see in the garden
the horse eating the lettuce.
At the Sleep Center
you said you slept better than at home.
It was your assignment.

Given an assignment you always ran with it.
Always a good student, you.
This house, this house is where we are now.
It's engraved on us and we on it.

When We Lived in Boulder

I remember seeing
a pregnant wild hog crossing the road.
She scampered into the underbrush.
Fire of sticks and dead grass
was burning on that nearby boulder.
She had to be running from it.
We all know when to run—or should.
Spring was soon to come with ducks.
Snowdrop tears, running deer, curious loons.

Rocks and stones asleep in the earth.
Our trees of rusty leaves in the yard
playing their spring accordions.

Camping

I am sure you remember
the time we went camping
and we were in front of our tent
making supper
over a fire of sticks
when two men, dirty in rags,
came quickly walking by us.
They spoke kindly and kept going.
You said if they come back and rape me,
don't try to stop them.
They might kill you.

So, was I to stand there and watch,
or cover my eyes?
Were you sewing seeds of sorrow
before Sorrow found you?

Well, they didn't come back.
And we both thought they would,
didn't we?
I picked up a crooked stick
and threw it on the fire.
My grandmother used to say crooked things
are not always crooked.

You Are Smiling at Yourself in the Mirror

Give that same smile to me.
I give you my word, my trust, all that I know.
You say, "All knowledge is reduced to probability."
You've made a leap to Hume's resolve.
Forget Hume! What about our love, even our lust?
I'm here trying to get through the night *and* day.
Anyway, it started out to be about *love*, you see.
How much does one have to depend on candlelight?
There is no answer in war or hyperbole or contraction.
I complained about your room. You said you don't love me.
That is how it started: a minor infraction.
You said in what looks like disorder is harmony.
True, but you can't be morose *and* grandiose.
Choose your walking shoes. We have a long way to go.

Wolf

The commuter drifts in and docks.
Hundreds of peasant farmers disembark.
Now they're crowding into the cathedral.
On their dusty knees, with praying hands,
they pray for an end to the fighting.
The mental fungus of unspeakable things.
Up in the hills a revolutionary gazes
into his pocket mirror, admiring himself.
Yet, at times the city seems normal.
Someone flushes a toilet;
someone takes the garbage out.
For no known reason a dress in a closet
falls from a hanger.
A mother again shows off
the trophy her son won in high school.
The commuter to the safe island
leaves without you.
Watching it go
you listen to the gunfire in the hills.

Calm Waters

The stream runs low under the grass
till it gets to the first bridge underpass,
where the bus stops.
We follow the stream.
It is like following sentences in a story.
On the way we pass quietly under a second bridge;
emerging,
we see a girl on the embankment.
She looks up at us, closing her book,
and gazes in wonderment
at the three of us.
She has stopped at the place where,
with a sense of pride,
as a wedge against disapproval,
a young man walks into the dark
interior of his family cottage,
making out dimly faces
of sternness and weeping,
escorting his new bride
followed by a handyman
carrying on his shoulder
her dowry in a heavy box.

1596

Walking through the village center
everyone expects to see men hanging on gibbets,
but today on a gibbet hangs a black woman.
Her dead body is secured to the pole
by ropes across her upper and lower body.
By wrapping a rope around the lower part
of her dress, securing it tightly to her legs,
the villagers have made an attempt to preserve
at least some vestige of her dignity
from the village thrill seekers.
Some say she killed, killed violently.
She's now slumped in sunlight rotting,
casting a heavy, heavy shadow.
No one kneels before her, weeping.
A hawk stands on her shoulder
looking about, making sure he's safe
before starting his work
at her wide-open eyes.

Fear and the City

From some unknown force
the street itself rippled,
shaking apart its stone slab grates,
its columns, its rails,
its electric cables, shaking
its wrecking cranes and its tramways,
its green lights, its red lights
hanging from their poles.
Where is the sequence,
where is the consequence?
People running, howling.
A bad movie or bad dream?
Traffic. Shaking bumper to bumper
at a standstill seemingly forever.
Rental cars all smashed in a ditch.
Fuel pumps littering the streets.
People everywhere screaming.
Streets with gaping cement holes
grew wider and deeper.
Gutters sent up the smell of dead rats,
dead gangsters, rotting
in their large wool coats.
All floating on a stream of waste
below the stalled subway.
All without sequence, without consequence.

Rain

You're sitting in the wicker chair by the window
reading a novel a thousand pages long.

Raindrops hitting the house like bullets.

In the city we know people are miserable,
crossing wet streets in front of cars
stopped at red lights,
impatiently waiting to go.

Smoke

My sister at fifteen used to slip into the garden,
pretending to tend the roses,
while drawing deeply on a cigarette,
blowing the smoke into the thicket of underbrush.
When the smoke rose through clusters of branches
and leaves, it rose in patterns
of roses about to open.

In China

I must have been five
when I asked my mother
if chickens have penises.
Around a red wheelbarrow
a scattering of white chickens
scratching and clucking
in a stretch of grass. Somewhere
in China a specialty restaurant
serves only penises—fried,
boiled, sautéed, grilled,
baked—any way
your taste dictates.

Don't Slam the Door on Your Way Out

Looking at her backside in the mirror,
she said, I hate my big ass.
I said, For some women a big ass is an asset.
She said, Don't make fun.
No joke, I said, I'm serious. Think about it.
For some it's almost religious.
Women in fancy cars with bucket seats.
Think about those royal goddesses
perched on painted iron.
And what about certain movie stars?
You see them all the time at retreats.
And that's when she slammed the door
on her way out.

Self and Self

Looking at himself suspiciously, carefully.
Looking at himself forgivingly.
Looking with detachment at himself
    and meaning it.
Sick, seeing himself sick.
Self-scrutiny with objectivity.
Excitement and intensity:
    seeing self with shocked eyes.
Broken and soft spoken,
the self as broken and soft spoken.
He's better now, nothing to say, but better.
In his chair, he leans forward,
    eager to say his say.
He comes in from winter, takes off winter coat
    in yellow room with yellow light.
He feeds his dogs, feeds himself.
Friends are over. Friends surround his table.
He's able to speak, to say what he meant
    to say to friends in a friendly way.
His hair turns white.
Looking in the mirror at his eyes
    beginning to fade and burn.
He turns up lights.

Father

I was there looking for the house
where my father died.
An old neighborhood,
clean and orderly,
with flower gardens flanking each front door.
Windows covered with white lace,
behind which nobody seemed to live.
Thanks to a restless cloudy sky,
a gray light hung over it all.
Despite the road sweeper's efforts
to smooth it over,
the main road was unpaved
and bore carriage tracks and car tracks.
And when I found the house,
at the deep end of the street, I knocked.
A woman came to the door
and said, Yes, he lives here
like a character in a gothic novel.
You see, when the storm came
and broke the levee, flooding the city,
leaving hundreds dead,
thousands stranded,
beach chairs and canopies blown away,
your father was a hero.
He got everyone out.
I knew it was a lie, but it was what I needed to hear.

Your Sister

Your big sister loves to comb your hair,
tie your shoes,
dress you as if you were a helpless child.
You're late, but your bags are packed,
your ticket in your pocket,
and your sister insists on once again
combing your hair, just for the road,
parting it, combing it one way, then another.
You love it, and you hate it.
This won't take but a minute, she says.
With tweezers your sister pulls random hairs
from your chin, your neck, and your ears,
showing her affection, making sure
you are Perfection as you set out
on your trip, perhaps your last.

Your Aunt

Your only living relative,
your aunt, is in your dressing room
to wish you well, to express her love for you,
before you go out there to face them.
You tell her
it's not like you're going off to war.
She hugs you,
stands back holding you by your padded shoulders,
and straightens your lapels.
She takes your face in her hands,
gently shaking your head,
telling you she's your only living relative,
your mother's sister.
Family, she says, is love.
Your dear girlfriend, on a swivel stool
in the corner across the room,
keeping her eyes averted,
nervously turning from side to side,
quietly smiling to herself.

And you are beginning to doubt,
to fear for something
you never thought about till now.

The Mall: 50% Off Day

A girl with dimples tucks up her skirt. Barefoot,
she tiptoes down the path, carrying
a handful of grain. She comes out to the edge
of the creek, where on a rock I'm reading
Emily's poems, dreaming her dreams
and living her schemes in between
her arbitrary dashes. And just then the girl,
with her own crafty plot, throws the grain out
into the ripples of the water to feed the ducks.
With greed they move at a ripping speed,
gaining advantage, moving each other aside,
pecking and pulling,
bumping for the best position.

The Tourist

She lifts both arms
as if she's inventing the first day.
You're the thread; she's the needle.

> *The naked smell of hair*
> *under a woman's arms.*

Once the day is spent, with a headache
you're back in the hotel room.

Because of bad weather
all flights
except hers are grounded.

The Longing

And then it happens: up is down.
She slips, she falls—
    not into the water
    but into the sky.
It's a warm day,
    but snow is still piled
    on limbs of pine
    as she floats up.
She opens her umbrella
    and drifts higher and higher.
You watch with both
    disappointment and amazement.

She is almost not there, but there she is,
    a dot in the sky over the sea.
She is the girl you loved a lot.

She is the one you remember.

Girl Spinning

True, I'm attracted to her.
Long-legged girl
on a low stool hunching over her spinning wheel,
working the treadle with her foot,
spinning wool into yarn.
There is dancing here in the spinning
and the turning of the wheel.
I can tell she feels the pleasure of the wheel;
she feels it in her legs, she feels it in her arms,
she feels it in the staying power
of the wheel itself spinning
to the rhythm of itself
and the rhythm of her body
wedding itself to the wheel.
I'm feeling the pleasure of her.
I want to say, May I have this dance?

The Unknown

From the porch I watch the barefoot boy
with the watering can walking the garden rows,
watering the rosebushes along the fence.
There's symmetry, there's unity,
yet I feel the presence of helplessness in things,
the succumbing of the prey to the predator.
And I rethink Blake and his unknown.
As the boy makes progress,
I stress and ponder the future roses.
Will they come up to our approval?
And if not who are we to disapprove?
Will the roses light up our dining table?
Will they crystallize our plans?
So we approve or disapprove. Why bother?
From the porch I wait like a gentleman
at the door of a Paris brothel.

Urgent Care

In the waiting room I wait.
Across from me a little girl with a broken arm.
Her mother, seven feet tall in jeans,
grew up on a ranch. When her son says
he saw a chicken walk around with no head,
she says, Chickens do that all the time.
I saw a whole bunch of them do that.

I go in to see the doctor,

and when I come out, they are gone,
replaced by an old couple,
side by side,
facing a mirror, reflecting their misery.
Her lipstick slightly smeared,
a hat shading her swollen eyes.

Surrey

Once upon a time
a team of horses in the rain
on a gloomy day
pulling a surrey black as a hearse
up a muddy road
toward a house
at the top,

passing a rusting plow
standing upright in mud,

and just as they pass,
the plow falls over—
plop—
into the soft, upturned earth.

Bronze

From the shadows that morning
I saw the priest open the side door,
and hordes of peasant women and children
pried in hoping to kiss the sacred relic.
The priest held it with both hands, and
in single file each believer kissed
the bronze object,
each miserable face reflecting dimly
in the tarnished unvarnished surface.
I watched in amazement,
then slipped out unseen, safely
back into my sinful life.

Sky and Marble

A dog from nowhere starts barking,
and my horse throws me

and runs off downhill

while I lay broken flat on my back
unable to move.

Down the road
the Five-Fifteen groans by,
bringing commuters back from the city.

As I lie here facing the sky,
I remember
the day I hid behind the marble folds
of the Virgin's flowing garments

while my mother desperately searched
the museum for her lost boy.

Clawing

I'm glad we had coffee together today
at the outdoor café.
We once loved each other.
This is what I wanted to say to you
but couldn't find the words.
Obsessed with your own childhood,
believing your mother never understood,
your father didn't care,
you now test yourself with impossible puzzles,
over and over you work them
upside down and sideways and in the dark
to make sure your score defeats you
because it must, it must.
Just as the jerk in the crowd is for you
always the attraction and the easiest to spot.
This one you never miss.
Sail on, happy girl, sail on!
You are a continuous sentence,
the period of which will come
in the form of your clinched fist
holding an introduction letter
from yourself to yourself.

Together

They make the bed together.
They grocery shop together.
She finds his lost sock.
If she shells the peas, he washes them
and trims the trees.
She gathers the leaves.

With both wings clasped together,
the woman holds the rooster
firmly against her apron
as it squawks and squawks.
Her husband waiting with the hatchet
at the chopping block.

Evening Newspaper

Going home on the subway,
when you open the newspaper
you'd just picked up
at the corner
before coming down the steps,
there is always the person
next to you slyly reading
over your shoulder
and getting visibly upset
when you turn the page
before they finish the story
about some woman in Mexico or Brazil
discovering the Virgin's face in a mango
or seeing it in a puddle of water
in the road to the junkyard
or the Granada dig uncovering the bones
of people fallen in their tracks
during attacks in a medieval street battle.
Keep turning.

Rush Hour

Hot and wet
and in the rudeness of the crowd
we're rushing along
holding on to our
    uncontrolable umbrellas.
We're dreaming of a different horizon.
We're dreaming
of having no particular place
    to go,
dreaming of strolling easily
    under evergreens
heavy
with piles of snow.

The Argument

After the argument the two sit
back to back.
Bit by bit they make up.
They swim out to the big rock.

They search for clams.

They check on the horse.
The argument seems so long ago.
The horse eats out of their hands.

They cross the yard.

He pushes her in the swing,
up and back,

but at the dinner table

the argument comes back,
saying, Here I am.
Play me like a violin.

Early Bird

Everybody on the bus seems to be asleep
except the driver,
with his great staying power,

and me. The sun is rising
as we approach.
Two warring armies coming face-to-face
on the pages of a comic book.

And we enter the city.
A foggy morning under elevated tracks.
In shop lights not yet turned off

a lone woman
in a tight red dress
holding over her head a black umbrella.

She smiles and waves to the bus.
I wave back,
as if I'm one of the soldiers
ready to surrender.

Strangers on the Train

I board the train.
I enter a third-class car.
A guard sitting beside a young woman.

Her left hand cuffed to his right.
She hangs her head sadly.

The train shakes,
bangs twice, three times,
then starts rolling
uneasily, unsteadily.

Now moving faster,
gaining in smoothness.

We enter a tunnel.

The interior lights go out.
Total blackness. Tunnel echo.

We exit, shooting out
to the glare of sunlight.

I hear the prisoner
saying,
I have to go to the toilet.

Cyclops

Coming around the corner a hearse
easing its way into the festivities,

causing a maze,
dispersing dancers and prancing girls,
cutting off marchers,
teams of drummers and horn blowers.

Defying us to be happy.

The driver winking at us
his one big eye.

Perfume

We were in the breakfast café
of a little, out-of-the-way hotel in Paris
when he came in,
his perfume preceding him
filling the whole room.

There were others there—
an English family of four,
two young German guys,
three American college girls.
Everyone stopped eating.
The girls tried to suppress a giggle.
The two English kids
openly held their noses.

It was truly suffocating.
Presently the servicer came
with his pot of coffee and hot milk.

Later you said we should be grateful
for his perfume. I wouldn't want
to imagine what it was concealing.

On Watching a Caterpillar Become a Butterfly

It's a slow, slow process
sitting here on the porch

watching a clumsy caterpillar

slowly turning itself
into a graceful butterfly while

hanging from the underside
of a withered leaf dark with life,

a leaf among a pungent cluster
of other leaves, hanging

from this old branch,
leaning over my banister.

At a certain point
in its natural growth

caterpillar thinks it can
decide which way

to go—to fly or die—
by simply dreaming

of having the loveliness
of the crow butterfly,

or having the stripes
of the tiger butterfly,

or staying in the chrysalis stage,
or becoming a friar butterfly.

Caterpillar is a dreamer
and a natural schemer.

In this changing light where
cuticle-shaped drops of fluid

glow and glow
like red nectar,

he is changing himself
as he hangs from the bottom

of this green leaf,
wedged tightly

as though bolted
with metal springs.

He throws off light,
a light of silver,

outlined in gold,
with gold trimmings.

Le Port Nice

The boats
are all clustered

in the port
like Valerie's thirsty puppies

around a bowl of milk
lapping and whining.

The boats have names
like Ramona and Renata,

Redella and Rolanda,
Lena and Marcellina.

Like the puppies
the boats nudge and bounce

against each other
making puppy noises.

And after a leisurely lunch
the trusty sailors

will come down
the old Roman road

to pet and pamper
their boats

before setting them out
to sail.

This Is Becoming a Trend

Last week windows replaced.
Doors next, I bet.

With sweat dripping
into their work

the floor strippers
finished yesterday.

The new varnish
still partly wet.

This is the season
of spring cleaning.

We're trapped outside
in the yard,

looking in
like dogs

locked out
for good reason.

El Greco Comes Home

We were in Greece,
but for a moment

it looked like Spain.
A ship too large to come into bay

coming in anyway,
and as far as I could see

a sort of El Greco *Toledo*
in the distance,

with dark clouds
dancing

in a sky black
with green rain,

and trees trembling
at their base,

shaken from the ground
by wind

and given a good thrashing
as if they had sinned.

Color of the Wind

It was a tightrope night.
Long day of readings, translations, and signings.
We were all in Rotterdam for the poetry festival.
At dinner at a sidewalk café,
lots of beer on the table,

new friend Jonathan, from London,
started his rant saying he didn't understand poetry.
This is all a lot of nonsense.
You blokes, he said—meaning all five of us—
are probably pretending to understand.

Some of us were appalled. You took a stand.
You said, To get it, you can't lose hope.
It's about rejoicing in life.
You said, It's like Maxwell Bodenheim said:
it's an "attempt to paint the color of the wind."
Jon said, Who the hell is Maxwell Bodenheim?
One has to face the guillotine
without losing one's head—
That's when I jumped in.
I don't remember exactly
but I said something like
Jon apparently never felt
the top of his head taken off.

Some of us lost our poise.
Too much noise and beer.
The sun down hours ago
but the sky still full of daylight.

Look at the sky, you said.
It's night and day at the same time.
Then you proposed a toast to Los—
the beating of our hearts.